1001

KNOCK

KNOCK

JOKES

D0932364

1001 KNOCK KNOCK JOKES

Jasmine Birtles

Robinson
London

Robinson Publishing Ltd
7 Kensington Church Court
London W8 4SP

First published by Robinson Children's Books,
an imprint of Robinson Publishing Ltd 1998

This collection copyright © Robinson Publishing 1998

Cover illustrations copyright © Julek Heller 1998

All rights reserved. This book is sold subject to the condition that it
shall not, by way of trade or otherwise, be lent, re-sold, hired out or
otherwise circulated in any form of binding or cover other than that in
which it is published and without a similar condition including this
condition being imposed on the subsequent purchaser.

ISBN 1 85487 868 9

A copy of the British Library Cataloguing-in-Publication Data is
available from the British Library

Printed and bound in the E.C.

10 9 8 7 6 5 4 3 2 1

Introduction

Knock knock

Who's there?

Joke Book

Joke Book Who?

Joke Book full of fantastic knock knock jokes
- that's who! Yes this is the biggest, the best, the most
brilliant knock knock joke book in the world! If you have this
book of knock knock jokes you will always be able to tell
someone a joke. In fact, by the time you've finished reading
this book you should be able to make up your own knock knock
jokes. Go on! I dare you. Go round your house making up knock
knock jokes about anything you see - knife, fork, spoon, chair,
nintendo, hi-fi or anything else. I have included as many girls'
and boys' names as I could think of but if I haven't included
yours or your friend's then write and tell me. I'll include it
in the next one. or you could send me your own knock knock
joke based on a name I haven't used. I always write back to
anyone who sends me a letter and I would be happy to hear
from you. So get knock knocking and make all your friends and
family laugh with your cracking jokes.

Knock knock.

Who's there?

Jasmine Birtles.

Jasmine Birtles who?

Jasmine Birtles wrote these jokes so if you
like them write and tell her so

Jasmine Birtles

c/o Robinson Publishing Ltd

7 Kensington Church Court

London W8 4SP

Knock knock.

Who's there?
Xena.
Xena who?
Xena minute!

Knock knock.
Who's there?
Etta.
Etta who?
Etta boy!

Knock knock.
Who's there?
Tilly.
Tilly who?
Tilly cows come home.

Knock knock.
Who's there?
Kristin.
Kristin who?
Kristining robe.

Knock knock

Knock knock.
Who's there?
Audrey.
Audrey who?
Audrey another drink.

Who's there?
Rena.
Rena who?
Renamok in the
shopping mall.

Knock knock.
Who's there?
Ellen.
Ellen who?
Ellen high water.

Knock knock.
Who's there?
Pammy.
Pammy who?
Pammy something
nice when you are at
the shops!

Knock knock.
Who's there?
Eunice.
Eunice who?
Eunice is like your
nephew.

Knock knock.
Who's there?
Cecile.
Cecile who?
Cecile the envelope.

Knock knock.
Who's there?
Rosina.
Rosina who?
Rosina vase.

Knock knock.
Who's there?
Elly.
Elly who?
Ellymentary, my dear Watson.

Knock knock.
Who's there?
Phoebe.
Phoebe who?
Phoebe way above
my price.

Knock knock.
Who's there?
Janet.
Janet who?
Janet a big fish?

Knock knock.
Who's there?
Grace.
Grace who?
Grace skies are
over us.

Knock knock.
Who's there?
Sherry.
Sherry who?
Sherry trifle!

Knock knock.
Who's there?
Augusta.
Augusta who?
Augustalmost felt
like winter.

Knock knock.
Who's there?
Gertie.
Gertie who?
Gertiesy call!

Knock knock.
Who's there?
Enid.
Enid who?
Enid some food now!

Knock
knock.
Who's
there?
olive.
olive who?
olive in
this house
 - what
are you
doing
there?

Knock knock.
Who's there?
Peg.
Peg who?
Peg your pardon, I've
got the wrong door.

Knock knock.
Who's there?
Dana.
Dana who?
Dana you mind.

Knock knock.
Who's there?
Aida.
Aida who?
Aida whole sandwich
at lunchtime.

Knock knock.
Who's there?
Cynthia.
Cynthia who?
Cynthia won't listen
I'll keep shouting.

Knock knock.
Who's
there?
Shelby.
Shelby who?
(sing) "Shelby
coming round
the mountain
when she comes".

Knock knock.
Who's there?
Norma.
Norma who?
Normally
the butler
opens the
door.

Who's there?

Tina who?

Knock knock.
Who's there?
Fiona.
Fiona who?
Fiona large house and
a car.

Knock knock.
Who's there?
Marie.
Marie who?
Marie for love.

Knock knock.
Who's there?
Mae.
Mae who?
(sing) "Mae be it's
because I'm a
Londoner".

Knock knock.
Who's there?
Marietta.
Marietta who?
Marietta whole loaf!

Knock knock.
Who's there?
Roxie.
Roxie who?
Roxie Horror
Show.

Knock knock.
Who's there?
Amy.
Amy who?
Amy for the
top.

Knock knock.
Who's there?
Maya.
Maya who?
Maya turn.

Knock knock.
Who's there?
Ruth.
Ruth who?
Ruthless people.

Knock knock.
Who's there?
Iris.
Iris who?
Iris you would
open the door.

Knock knock.
Who's there?
Cassie.
Cassie who?
Cassie you some
time?

Knock knock.
Who's there?
Willa.
Willa who?
Willa present make you
happy?

Knock knock.
Who's there?
Edna.
Edna who?
Edna Cloud.

Knock knock.
Who's there?
Elizabeth.
Elizabeth who?
Elizabeth of
knowledge is a
dangerous thing.

Knock knock.
Who's there?
Bella.
Bella who?
Bella the ball.

Knock knock.
Who's there?
Marian.
Marian who?
Mariand her little
lamb.

Knock knock.
Who's there?
Martha.
Martha who?
Martha boys next door are hurting me!

Knock knock.
Who's there?
Alma.
Alma who?
Almany times do I have to knock?

Knock knock.
Who's there?
Dorothy.
Dorothy who?
(sing) "Dorothynk I'm sexy?"

Knock knock.
Who's there?
Dot.
Dot who?
Dotty about you.

Knock knock.
Who's there?
Doris.
Doris who?
Dorisk a cream cake
- it won't hurt you.

Knock knock.
Who's there?
May.
May who?
Maybe it's a friend
at the door.

Knock knock.
Who's there?
Judy.
Judy who?
Judyliver
newspapers still?

Knock knock.
Who's there?
Jade.
Jade who?
Jade a whole pie
today.

Knock knock.
Who's there?
Amber.
Amber who?
Amberter than I
was yesterday.

Knock knock.
Who's there?
Sophia.
Sophia who?
Sophia nothing...fear
is pointless.

Knock knock.
Who's there?
Carlene.
Carlene who?
Carlene against
that wall!

Knock knock.
Who's there?
Camilla.
Camilla who?
Camilla minute!

Knock knock.
Who's there?
Denise.
Denise who?
Denise are above de
feet.

Knock knock.
Who's there?
Nancy.
Nancy who?
Nancy a piece of
cake?

Knock knock.
Who's there?
Vanessa.
Vanessa who?
Vanessa time I'll
ring the bell.

Knock knock.
Who's there?
Winnie.
Winnie who?
Winnie is better
than losing.

Knock knock.
Who's there?
Isla
Isla who?
Isla be seeing you!

Knock knock.
Who's there?
Samantha.
Samantha who?
Samantha baby have
gone for a walk.

Knock knock.
Who's there?
Della.
Della who?
Della tell ya that I
love ya?

Knock knock.
Who's there?
Louise.
Louise who?
Louise coming to tea
today.

Knock knock.

Who's there?
Clara.
Clara who?
Clara space on the
table.

Knock knock.
Who's there?
Penny.
Penny who?
Penny for your
thoughts.

Knock knock.
Who's there?
Bridie.
Bridie who?
Bridie light of the
silvery moon.

Knock knock.
Who's there?
Olivia.
Olivia who?
Olivia'l is great for
cooking.

Knock knock.
Who's there?
Briony.
Briony who?
Briony, beautiful sea.

Knock knock.
Who's there?
Daryl.
Daryl who?
Daryl be the day.

Knock knock.
Who's there?
Bettina.
Bettina who?
Bettina minute you'll
    let me in.

Knock knock.
Who's there?
Carolyn.
Carolyn who?
Carolyn of rope with
you.

Knock knock.
Who's there?
Claudette.
Claudette who?
Claudette a whole
cake.

Knock knock.
Who's there?
Meg.
Meg who?
Meg a fuss.

Knock knock.
Who's there?
Justine.
Justine who?
Justine case.

Annabel.
Annabel who?
Annabel would be useful on this door.

Ava.
Ava who?
Ava good mind to leave you.

Nicky.
Nicky who?
Nicky nacks.

Stephanie.
Stephanie who?
Stephanie gas - we need to go faster!

Hazel.
Hazel who?
Hazel restrict your
vision.

Gail.
Gail who?
Gail of laughter.

Jeanette.
Jeanette who?
Jeanette has too many
holes in it, the bigger
fish will escape.

Tori.
Tori who?
Tori I upset you.

Knock knock.
Who's there?
Tracy.
Tracy who?
Tracy the shape in pencil.

Knock knock.
Who's there?
Cindy.
Cindy who?
Cindy parcel special delivery.

Knock knock.
Who's there?
Jan.
Jan who?
Jan and bread.

Knock knock.
Who's there?
Marcia.
Marcia who?
Marcia me!

Knock knock.
Who's there?
Grace.
Grace who?
Graced my knee.

Knock knock.
Who's there?
Bertha.
Bertha who?
Bertha day boy.

Knock knock.
Who's there?
Leslie.
Leslie who?
Leslie town now
before they catch
us.

Knock knock.
Who's there?
Nell.
Nell who?
Nelly the
elephant.

Knock knock.
Who's there?
Renata.
Renata who?
Renata sugar. Can I borrow some?

Knock knock.
Who's there?
Audrey.
Audrey who?
Audrey lots of water every day.

Knock knock.
Who's there?
Rose.
Rose who?
Rose early one morning.

Knock knock.
Who's there?
Delphine.
Delphine who?
Delphine fine, thanks.

Knock knock.
Who's there?
Lucy.
Lucy who?
Lucylastic can let you down.

Knock knock.
Who's there?
Kiki.
Kiki who?
Kiki's stuck in the locklock - let me inin.

Knock knock.
Who's there?
Fifi.
Fifi who?
Fifiling c-cold, p-please I-let m-me in.

Knock knock.
Who's there?
Flossie.
Flossie who?
Flossie your teeth every day.

Knock knock.
Who's there?
Flo.
Flo who?
Flo your candles
out.

Knock knock.
Who's there?
Althea.
Althea who?
Althea in court.

Knock knock.
Who's there?
Evie.
Evie who?
Evie weather.

Knock knock.
Who's there?
Effie.
Effie who?
Effie'd known you were coming he'd have stayed home.

Knock knock.
Who's there?
Hope.
Hope who?
Hope you'll have me.

Knock knock.
Who's there?
Yvette.
Yvette who?
Yvette helps lots of animals.

Knock knock.
Who's there?
Maia.
Maia who?
Maianimals are like children to me.

Who's there?

Avis who?

Knock knock.
Who's there?
Megan.
Megan who?
Megan a loud noise.

Knock knock.
Who's there?
Olga.
Olga who?
Olga home now.

Knock knock.
Who's there?
Stella.
Stella who?
Stella lot from the
rich people.

Knock knock.
Who's there?
Trudy.
Trudy who?
Trudy your word.

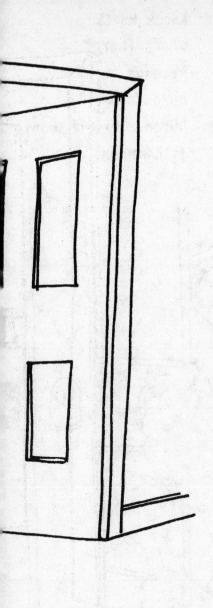

Knock knock.
Who's there?
Imogen.
Imogen who?
Imogenuine person.

Knock knock.
Who's there?
Phyllis.
Phyllis who?
Phyllis up.

Knock knock.
Who's there?
Anais.
Anais who?
Anais cup of tea.

Knock knock.
Who's there?
Lotte.
Lotte who?
Lotte sense.

Knock knock.
Who's there?
Julie.
Julie who?
Julie'n on this door a lot?

Knock knock.
Who's there?
Miranda.
Miranda who?
Miranda friend want to come in.

Knock knock.
Who's there?
Portia.
Portia who?
Portia the door - it's
stuck.

Knock knock.
Who's there.
Nadia.
Nadia who?
Nadia head if you
want to come in.

Knock knock.
Who's there?
olive.
olive who?
olive to regret it.

Knock knock.
Who's there?
Tilly.
Tilly who?
Tilly learns to say
please, he'll stay
outside.

Knock
knock.
Who's there?
felicity.
felicity who?
felicity getting more
polluted every day.

Knock knock.
Who's there?
Patty.
Patty who?
Patty-cake.

31

Knock knock.
Who's there?
Rita.
Rita who?
Rita novel.

Knock knock.
Who's there?
Rhona.
Rhona who?
Rhonaround town.

Knock knock.
Who's there?
Rhonda.
Rhonda who?
Rhonda why?

Knock knock.
Who's there?
Sandy.
Sandy who?
Sandy shore.

Knock knock.
Who's there?
Kim.
Kim who?
Kim too late.

Knock knock.
Who's there?
Pam.
Pam who?
Pamper yourself.

Knock knock.
Who's there?
Theresa.
Theresa who?
Theresa green.

Kathy you again?

Knock knock. Who's there?
Lacey. Lacey who?
Lacey crazy days.

Knock knock.
Who's there?
India.
India who?
India there's a bag
belonging to me.

Knock knock.
Who's there?
Iona.
Iona who?
Iona house of my
own, you know.

Knock knock.
Who's there?
Lana.
Lana who?
Lana the free.

Knock knock.
Who's there?
Lily.
Lily who?
Lily-livered varmint!

Knock knock.
Who's there?
Lee.
Lee who?
Lee've it to me.

Knock knock.
Who's there?
Leah.
Leah who?
Leahn egg for my tea.

Who's there?

Courtney who?

Knock Knock

Knock knock.
Who's there?
Jacqueline.
Jacqueline who?
Jacqueline Hyde.

Knock knock.
Who's there?
Lucetta.
Lucetta who?
Lucetta a difficult
problem.

Knock knock.
Who's there?
Leonie.
Leonie who.
Leonie one I love.

Knock knock.
Who's there?
Mandy.
Mandy who?
Mandy guns.

Knock knock.
Who's there?
Mamie.
Mamie who?
Mamie a new dress.

Knock knock.
Who's there?
Posie.
Posie who?
Posie hard questions.

Knock knock.
Who's there?
Petal.
Petal who?
Petal fast, we're
nearly there.

Knock knock.
Who's there?
Alice.
Alice who?
Alice on your new
house.

Knock knock.
Who's there?
Margo.
Margo who?
Margo, you're not
needed now.

Knock knock.
Who's there?
Mary.
Mary who?
That's what I keep
wondering.

Knock knock.
Who's there?
Maude.
Maude who?
Mauden living.

Knock knock.

Mavis

Mavis be
the best day
of your life.

Knock knock.
Who's there?
Meg.
Meg who?
Meg some toast. I'm
hungry.

Knock knock.
Who's there?
Minnie.
Minnie who?
Minnie people want to
come in.

Knock knock.
Who's there?
Joanna.
Joanna who?
Joanna smack? Let me
in.

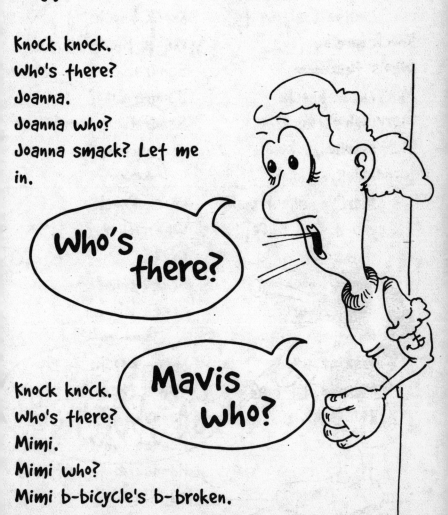

Who's there?

Mavis who?

Knock knock.
Who's there?
Mimi.
Mimi who?
Mimi b-bicycle's b-broken.

Knock knock.
Who's there?
Louise.
Louise who?
Louise waiting to
come in too.

——

Knock knock.
Who's there?
Marilyn.
Marilyn who?
Marilyn, she'll make
you a good wife.

——

Knock knock.
Who's there?
Maxine.
Maxine who?
Maxine a lot of
things.

Knock knock.
Who's there?
Maria.
Maria who?
Marial name

⊐

Knock knock.
Who's there?
Sandra.
Sandra who?
Sandrabout your toes
on the beach.

~~~~

Knock knock.
Who's there?
Greta.
Greta who?
Greta job.

o — o

Knock knock.
Who's there?
Hannah.
Hannah who?
Hannah cloth out, I'm
all dirty.

Knock knock.
Who's there?
Michelle.
Michelle who?
Michelle has sounds of the sea in it.

Knock knock.
Who's there?
Heather.
Heather who?
Heather pothtman
come yet?

Knock knock.
Who's there?
Heidi.
Heidi who?
Heidiclare war on
you.

Knock knock.
Who's there?
Hedda.
Hedda who?
Hedda ball in goal.

Knock knock.
Who's there?
Hester.
Hester who?
Hester la vista!

Knock knock.
Who's there?
Ida.
Ida who?
Ida bought a different
knocker if I'd been you.

Knock knock.
Who's there?
Ina.
Ina who?
Ina minute!

Knock knock.
Who's there?
Ines.
Ines who?
Inespecial place I'll hide your present.

Knock knock.
Who's there?
Francoise.
Francoise who?
Francoise once a great empire.

43

Knock knock.
Who's there?
Ingrid.
Ingrid who?
Ingrid sorrow I have
to leave you.

Knock knock.
Who's there?
Jackie.
Jackie who?
Jackie'n that job –
it's killing you.

Knock knock.
Who's there?
Juliet.
Juliet who?
Juliet him get away
with that?

Knock knock.
Who's there?
Juanita.
Juanita who?
Juanita big meal?

Knock knock.
Who's there?
Jenny.
Jenny who?
Jenny-d anything
from the shops?

Knock knock.
Who's there?
Jasmine.
Jasmine who?
Jasmine like to play
in bands.

Knock knock.
Who's there?
Jessica.
Jessica who?
Jessica lot up last
night?

Knock knock.
Who's there?
Fleur.
Fleur who?
Fleuride toothpaste.

~~~~~~~~~

Knock knock.
Who's there?
Poppy.
Poppy who?
Poppy'n any time you like.

Knock knock.
Who's there?
Daisy.
Daisy who?
Daisy that you are in,
but I don't believe them.

Knock knock.
Who's there?
Polly.
Polly who?
Polly the other one,
it's got bells on.

Knock knock.
Who's there?
Tania.
Tania who?
Tania self round, you'll
see.

Knock knock.
Who's there?
Dolly.
Dolly who?
Dolly't us in, we're
cold!

Knock knock.
Who's there?
Liz.
Liz who?
Liz see what you look
like.

"KNOCK

Nola.
Nola who?
Nolaner driver may
drive a car alone.

Katherine.
Katherine who?
Katherine together
for a social evening.

Lucille.
Lucille who?
Lucilleing is danger-
ous to live under.

Sue.
Sue who?
Sue'n you will know.

Sybil.
Sybil who?
Sybiling rivalry.

Eve.
Eve who?
Eve-ho, here we go.

June.
June who?
June know how to
open a door?

Fanny.
Fanny who?
Fanny you not know-
ing who I am!

49

KNOCK KNOCK

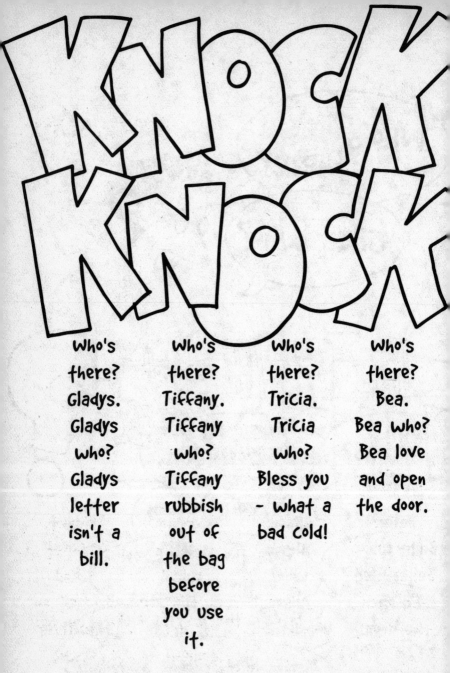

Who's
there?
Gladys.
Gladys
who?
Gladys
letter
isn't a
bill.

Who's
there?
Tiffany.
Tiffany
who?
Tiffany
rubbish
out of
the bag
before
you use
it.

Who's
there?
Tricia.
Tricia
who?
Bless you
- what a
bad cold!

Who's
there?
Bea.
Bea who?
Bea love
and open
the door.

ock knock. Knock knock. Knock knock. Knock Knock knock. knock.

WHO'S THERE?

Belle.	Alison.	Caitlin.	Bridget.
Belle who?	Alison who?	Caitlin who?	Bridget who?
Belle-t up and open the door.	Alison Wonderland.	Caitlin you my dress tonight - I'm wearing it.	Bridget on the River Kwai.

Knock knock.
Who's there?
Amber.
Amber who?
Ambersting to go to
the bathroom.

Knock knock.
Who's there?
Samantha.
Samantha who?
Samantha with you?

Knock knock.
Who's there?
Beth.
Beth who?
Beth foot forward.

Knock knock.

Candice

Candice be love?

Knock knock.
Who's there?
Bethany.
Bethany who?
Bethany good shows
recently?

Who's there?

Candice who?

Knock knock.
Who's there?
Bernadette.
Bernadette who?
Bernadette my dinner.

Knock knock.
Who's there?
Ada.
Ada who?
Ada lot for breakfast.

Knock knock.
Who's there?
Bette.
Bette who?
Bette of roses.

Knock knock.   Knock knock.   Knock knock.
Who's there?   Who's there?   Who's there?
Betty.   Alma.   Amanda.
Betty who?   Alma who?   Amanda who?
Betty earns a   Alma lovin'.   Amanda the
lot of money.   table.

Knock knock.
Who's there?
Juno.
Juno who?
Juno how to
get out of
here?

Knock knock.
Who's there?
Una.
Una who?
Yes, Una who.

Knock knock.
Who's there?
Carmen.
Carmen who?
Carmen like
best is a
Ferrari.

Who's there?

Knock
knock.
Who's
there?
Carrie.
Carrie
who?
Carrie on
with
what you
are doing.

Aileen who?

against my Rolls
-Royce

Knock knock.
Who's there?
Yvonne.
Yvonne who?
Yvonne to know vat
you are doing.

Knock knock.
Who's there?
Aurora.
Aurora who?
Aurora's just come
from a big lion!

Knock knock.
Who's there?
Celeste.
Celeste who?
Celeste time I come
calling.

Knock knock.
Who's there?
Vanda.
Vanda who?
Vanda you vant me to
come round?

Knock knock.
Who's there?
Violet.
Violet who?
Violet the cat out of
the bag.

Knock knock.
Who's there?
Joan.
Joan who?
Joan call us, we'll
call you.

Knock knock. - Who's there? - Shirley.
Shirley who? - Shirley you know who I am!

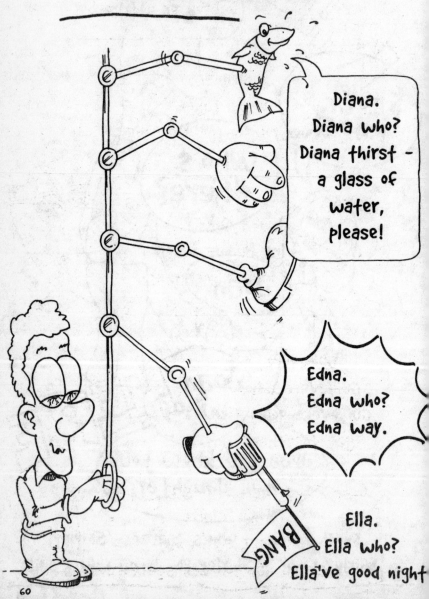

Debbie.
Debbie who?
Debbie or not to be

———— .

Donna.
Donna who?
Donna you know? Isa Luigi.

———— .

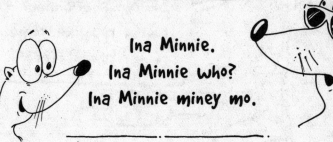

Ina Minnie.
Ina Minnie who?
Ina Minnie miney mo.

————

Guinevere.
Guinevere who?
Guinevere going to
get together?

Honor Claire.
Honor Claire who?
Honor Claire day you can see forever.

Knock knock

Sharon.
Sharon who?
Sharon share alike -
would you like some
of my chocolate?

Knock knock.
Who's there?
Lucinda.
Lucinda who?
(sing) "Lucinda sky
with diamonds ..."

Knock knock.
Who's there?
Sarah.
Sarah who?
Sarah doctor
in the house?

Knock knock.
Who's there?
Elsie.
Elsie who?
Elsie you in court!

Knock knock
Who's there?
Viola.
Viola who?
Viola sudden you don't
know who I am?

Who's there?

Knock knock.
Who's there?
Sonia.
Sonia who?
Sonia shoe -
it's stinking
the house out.

Knock knock.
Who's there?
Utica.
Utica who?
(sing) "Utica high road and
I'll take the low road."

Knock Knock. Who's there?...

Ivy.
Ivy who?
Ivyll cast a spell
on you.

Carol.
Carol who?
Carol go if you switch
the ignition on.

Aida.
Aida who?
Aida whole box
of chocolates
and I feel
really sick.

Emma.
Emma who?
Emma new resident here –
come round for tea.

Knock knock

Who's there?

Colleen.
Colleen who?
Colleen yourself up,
you're a mess!

Germaine.
Germaine who?
Germaine you don't
recognize me?

Bridget.
Bridget who?
Bridget the end
of the world.

Trudy.
Trudy who?
Trudy light from Turkey.

Knock knock
Who's there?

Barbara.
Barbara who?
(sing) "Barbara black sheep,
have you any wool?"

Knock knock.
Who's there?
Sigrid.
Sigrid who?
Sigrid Service.

Wendy.
Wendy who?
Wendy come to take you away
I won't stop them!

Knock knock.
Who's there?
Dawn.
Dawn who?
Dawn do anythi
I wouldn't do.

Knock knock.
Who's there?
Dionne.
Dionne who?
Dionne my last exam.

Knock knock.
Who's there?
Joan.
Joan who?
Joan rush, I'll tell you
in a minute.

Knock knock. Who's there?
Frances.
Frances who?
Frances on the other side
of the channel.

Knock knock.
Who's there?
Ina.
Ina who?
Ina minute I'm
going to knock
your door down.

WHO'S THERE?

Giselle.
Giselle who?
Gisellegant and
very pretty.

—

Barbie.
Barbie who?
Barbie Q.

onya.
onya who?
onya marks
get set
go.

Eva.
Eva who?
Eva had a smack
in the mouth?

Annette.
Annette who?
Annette curtain
looks good in the
window.

Knock knock.
Who's there?
Danielle.
Danielle who?
Danielle so loud – I heard
you the first time

Knock knock.
Who's there?
Anya.
Anya who?
Anya best behaviour.

Knock Knock

Joanna

Joanna **BIG** kiss?

Knock knock.
Who's there?
Gita.
Gita who?
Gita job!

Knock knock.
Who's there?
Aleta.
Aleta who?
Aleta bit of
lovin'.

Knock knock.
Who's there?
Annie.
Annie who?
Annie one you
like.

Knock knock.
Who's there?
Claudia.
Claudia who?
Claudia eyes,
out didn't I?

Who's there?

Joanna Who

Knock knock.
Who's there?
Liz.
Liz who?
Lizen carefully, I will
say this only once.

Knock knock.
Who's there?
Tamsin.
Tamsin who?
Tamsin time again I come
to the wrong house.

Knock knock.
Who's there?
Stacey.
Stacey who?
Stacey what happens
next.

Knock knock. Who's there? Sorrel. Sorrel who?
Sorrel about the mess.

Knock knock.
Who's there?
Maude.
Maude who?
Mauden my job's
worth.

Knock knock.
Who's there?
Saffron.
Saffron who?
Saffron a chair and it
collapsed.

Knock knock.
Who's there?
Julie.
Julie who?
Juliek official
secrets?

Knock knock.
Who's there?
Tara.
Tara who?
Tararaboomdeay.

Sacha.
Sacha who?
Sacha
money in
the bank.

Knock knock.
Who's there?
Corrinne.
Corrinne who?
Corrinne the bell now?

Knock knock.
Who's there?
Philippa.
Philippa who?
Philippa a bath - I'm
really dirty.

Knock knock.
Who's there?
Isabel.
Isabel who?
Isabel necessary on a
bicycle?

Knock knock.
Who's there?
Isadore.
Isadore who?
Isadore on the right
way round?

Knock knock.
Who's there?
Holly.
Holly who?
Hollylujah!

Knock knock.
Who's there?
Hans.
Hans who?
Hans across the sea.

Knock knock.
Who's there?
Pablo.
Pablo who?
Pablo the candles out.

Knock knock.
Who's there?
Aldo.
Aldo who?
Aldo the washing up
tonight.

Knock knock.
Who's there?
Sebastian.
Sebastian who?
Sebastian of society.

Knock knock.
Who's there?
Kevin.
Kevin who?
Kevin and sit down.

Knock knock.
Who's there?
Giuseppe.
Giuseppe who?
Giuseppe credit cards?

Knock knock.
Who's there?
Ron.
Ron who?
Ron answer.

Who's there?

Raymond who?

Knock knock.
Who's there?
Giovanni.
Giovanni who?
Giovanniny more
coffee?

Knock knock.
Who's there?
Al.
Al who?
Al be seeing you!

Knock knock.
Who's there?
Mikey.
Mikey who?
Mikey is stuck.

Knock knock.
Who's there?
Marvin.
Marvin who?
Marvin at
these
amazing
tricks.

Knock knock.
Who's there?
Abel.
Abel who?
Abel to see you, ha,
ha!

Knock knock.
Who's there?
Woody.
Woody who?
Woody come if we
asked him?

Knock knock.
Who's there?
Misha.
Misha who?
Misha lot of things
while I was away?

Knock knock.
Who's there?
Wilfred.
Wilfred who?
Wilfred come if we
ask nicely?

Knock knock.
Who's there?
Toby.
Toby who?
Toby or not Toby,
that is
the
question.

Knock knock.
Who's there?
Carl.
Carl who?
Carl you see?

Knock knock.
Who's there?
Sam.
Sam who?
Sam day you'll
recognize my voice.

Knock knock.
Who's there?
Huey.
Huey who?
Who am I? I'm me!

Knock knock.
Who's there?
Cyril.
Cyril who?
Cyril animals
at the zoo.

Knock knock.
Who's there?
Douglas.
Douglas who?
Douglas is
broken.

Knock knock.
Who's there?
Theodore.
Theodore who?
Theodore is
locked.

Knock knock.
Who's there?
Luther.
Luther who?
Luther please
- not tho
tight!

WHO'S THERE?

Knock knock. Who's there?

Knock knock.
Who's there?
Wade.
Wade who?
Wading room.

Knock knock.
Who's there?
Stefan.
Stefan who?
Stefan it!

Knock knock.
Who's there?
Patrick.
Patrick who?
Patricked me
into coming.

Eli. Eli who?

ELI ELI OH!!

Knock knock.
Who's there?
Alvin.
Alvin who?
Alvin zis com-
petition - just
vait and see!

Knock knock.
Who's there?
Ethan.
Ethan who?
Ethan all my
dinner.

Knock knock.
Who's there?
Raoul.
Raoul who?
Raoul of law.

Knock knock.
Who's there?
Saul.
Saul who?
Saul I know.

Knock knock.
Who's there?
Johann.
Johann who?
Johann! How
you doing, dude!

Knock knock.
Who's there?
Gus.
Gus who?
Gus what -
it's me!

Knock knock. Who's there?
Jess.
Jess who?
Don't know, you tell me.

Knock knock.
Who's there?
Costas.
Costas who?
Costas a
fortune to
get here.

Knock knock.
Who's there?
Herman.
Herman who?
Herman dry.

Knock knock.
Who's there?
Horatio.
Horatio who?
Horatio to the
end of the
road.

Knock knock. Who's there?
Franz.
Franz who?
Franz, Romans, countrymen, lend me your ears.

Knock knock.
Who's there?
Lloyd.
Lloyd who?
Lloyd him away with
an ice-cream.
◇

Knock knock.
Who's there?
Asa.
Asa who?
Asa glass of orange out
of the question?
◇

Knock knock.
Who's there?
Marcus.
Marcus who?
Marcus a
really nice boy.
◇

Knock knock.
Who's there?
Jerome.
Jerome who?
Jerome alone.
◇

Knock knock.
Who's there?
Aaron.
Aaron who?
Aaron the chest means
strength in arms.
◇

Knock knock.

Foster

Foster than a
speeding bullet.

Knock knock. Who's there?
Brian.
Brian who?
Brian drain!

Knock knock. Who's there?
Edwin.
Edwin who?

Edwin a cup if I could run faster.

Who's there?
Foster who?

Knock knock.
Who's there?
Walter.
Walter who?
Walter walter everywhere and not
a drop to drink.

Knock knock.   Knock knock.
Who's there?   Who's there?
Lester.   oliver.
Lester who?   oliver who?
Lester we forget.   oliver long way away.

Knock knock.
Who's there?
Vic.
Vic who?
Victory parade.

Knock knock.
Who's there?
Murphy.
Murphy who?
Murphy, murphy me!

Knock knock.
Who's there?
Arnie.
Arnie who?
Arnie going to let me in?

Knock knock.
Who's there?
Arnold.
Arnold who?
Arnold man.

Knock knock.
Who's there?
Thomas.
Thomas who?
Thomaster a language
takes a long time.

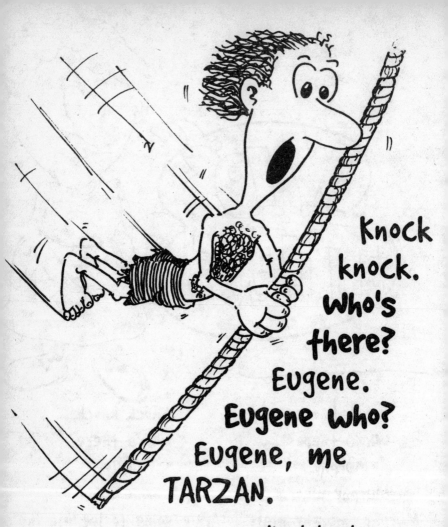

Knock
knock.
**Who's
there?**
Eugene.
Eugene who?
Eugene, me
TARZAN.

Knock knock.
Who's there?
Chester.
Chester who?
Chester minute! Don't you
know who I am?

Knock knock.
Who's there?
Barry.
Barry who?
Barry the dead.

Knock knock.
Who's there?
Clarence.
Clarence who?
Clarence Sale.

Knock knock.
Who's there?
Vincent.
Vincent who?
Vincent me here.

Knock knock.
Who's there?
Jamie.
Jamie who?
Jamie'n you don't recognize my voice?

Knock knock.
Who's there?
Cliff.
Cliff who?
Cliffhanger.

Knock knock.
Who's there?
Harry.
Harry who?
Harry up!

Knock knock.
Who's there?
Simon.
Simon who?
Simon time again I've told you not to do that.

Knock knock.
Who's there?
Fido.
Fido who?
Fido known you were coming I'd have baked a cake.

Knock knock.
Who's there?
York.
York who?
York, york, york.
This is funny.

Knock knock.
Who's there?
Mel.
Mel who?
Melt down!

Knock knock.
Who's there?
Alf.
Alf who?
Alf way home.

Knock knock.
Who's there?
Adair.
Adair who?
Adair you to open
this door.

Amos be mad! This isn't my house.

Knock knock.
Who's there?
Rudi.
Rudi who?
Rudi toot!

Knock knock.
Who's there?
Miles.
Miles who?
Miles away.

Knock knock.   Who's there?
Milo.   Milo who?
Milo bed is too uncomfortable.

Knock knock.
Who's there?
Jay.
Jay who?
Jay what you mean.

❧

Knock knock.
Who's there?
Howie.
Howie who?
Fine thanks. How are you?

❧ ❧

Knock knock.
Who's there?
Tim.
Tim who?
Tim after time.

❧ ❧ ❧

Knock knock.
Who's there?
Toto.
Toto who?
Totolly devoted to you.

Knock knock.
Who's there?
Max.
Max who?
Max Headroom.

Knock knock.
Who's there?
Craig.
Craig who?
Craig in the wall.

Knock knock.
Who's there?
Dave.
Dave who?
Dave of glory.

Knock knock.
Who's there?
Cohen.
Cohen who?
Cohen your way.

Knock knock.
Who's there?
Steve.
Steve who?
Steve upper lip.

Knock knock.
Who's there?
Reuben.
Reuben who?
Reuben my eyes.

Knock knock.
Who's there?
Jez.
Jez who?
Jezt a minute.

Knock knock.
Who's there?
Perry.
Perry who?
Perry well, thank you.

Knock knock.
Who's there?
Crispin.
Crispin who?
Crispin Crunchy is how I like my cereal.

Knock knock.
Who's there?
Tristan.
Tristan who?
Tristan elephant not to forget.

Knock knock.
Who's there?
Oscar.
Oscar who?
Oscar a foolish question, get a foolish answer.

Knock knock.
Who's there?
Robert.
Robert who?
Roberts are taking over the world.

Knock knock. Who's there?
Charles. Charles who?
Charles your luck on the roulette wheel.

Knock knock.
Who's there?
Mike.
Mike who?
Mike the best of it.

Knock knock.
Who's there?
Mark.
Mark who?
Mark my words.

Knock knock.
Who's there?
Michael.
Michael who?
Michaelock has stopped ticking.

Knock knock.
Who's there?
Roland.
Roland who?
Roland butter please.

Knock knock.
Who's there?
Julian.
Julian who?
Juliand I are going shopping now.

Knock knock.
Who's there?
Tariq,
Tariq who?
Tariq of perfume will put anyone off.

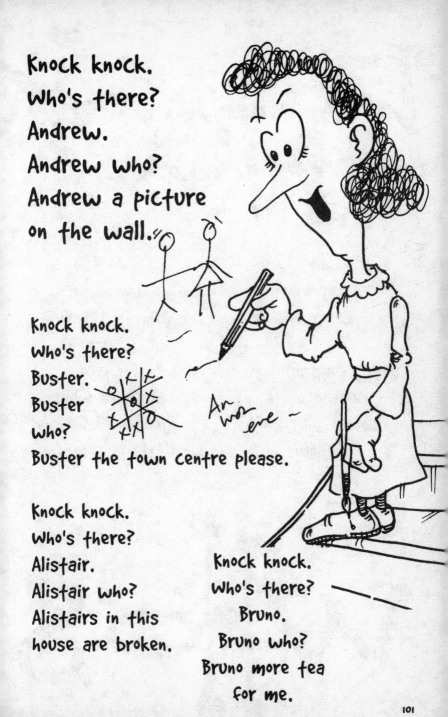

Knock knock.
Who's there?
Andrew.
Andrew who?
Andrew a picture
on the wall.

Knock knock.
Who's there?
Buster.
Buster
who?
Buster the town centre please.

Knock knock.
Who's there?
Alistair.
Alistair who?
Alistairs in this
house are broken.

Knock knock.
Who's there?
Bruno.
Bruno who?
Bruno more tea
for me.

101

Larry.
Larry who?
Larry up.

John.
John who?
John in the fun.

◇

Caesar.
Caesar who?
Caesar jolly good
fellow.

Richard.
Richard who?
Richard poor have
little in common.

KNOCK

James.
James who?
James people play.

Danny.
Danny who?
Dannybody home?

Laurie.
Laurie who?
Laurie-load of goods.

Chris.
Chris who?
Chrismas stocking.

THERE?

@

Knock knock.
Who's there?
Bill.
Bill who?
Bill of rights.
@ @
Knock knock.
Who's there?
francis.
francis who?
francis next to Germany.
@ @ @
Knock knock.
Who's there?
Tommy.
Tommy who?
Tommy you will always be beautiful.
@ @ @ @
Knock knock.
Who's there?
Dickon.
Dickon who?
Dickon the box with the right answer.

@ @ @ @ @

@

Knock knock.
Who's there?
Bernie.
Bernie who?
Bernie bridges.

@ @

Knock knock.
Who's there?
Philip.
Philip who?
Philip the car
with petrol.

@ @ @

@

Knock knock.
Who's there?
Callum.
Callum who?
Callum all back.

Knock knock.

Who's there?

Colin

Colin who?

Colin all cars.
Colin all cars...

Knock Knock

Duncan.
Duncan who?
Duncan biscuit
in your tea.

Scott.
Scott who?
Scott nothing
to do with you.

Egbert.
Egbert who?
Egbert no
bacon.

Ringo.
Ringo who?
Ringof
truth.

Ike.
Ike who?
Ike'n see
you
through
the
keyhole.

Who's there?

Cosmo.
Cosmo who?
Cosmo trouble than
you're worth.

Bobby.
Bobby who?
Bobbyn up and down
like this.

Knock knock.
Who's there?
Lionel.
Lionel who?

Lionel roar if you
stand on its tail.

Knock knock.
Who's there?
Atilla.
Atilla who?
Atilla you no lies.

Knock knock.
Who's there?
Abel.
Abel who?
Abel to go to work.

Knock knock.
Who's there?
Freddie.
Freddie who?
Freddie won't come out to play today.

Knock knock.
Who's there?
Len.
Len who?
Len us a fiver will you?

Knock knock. Who's there?
Adam.

Adam who?
Adam will burst
any minute
now.

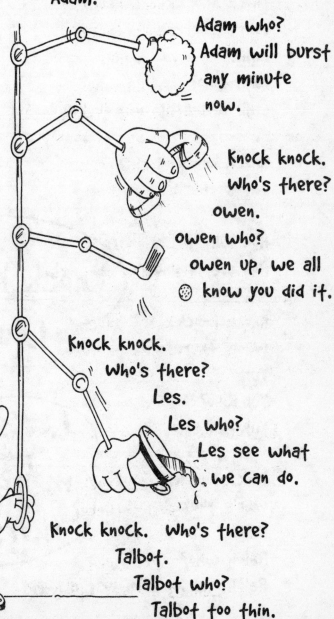

Knock knock.
Who's there?
Owen.
Owen who?
Owen up, we all
know you did it.

Knock knock.
Who's there?
Les.
Les who?
Les see what
we can do.

Knock knock. Who's there?
Talbot.
Talbot who?
Talbot too thin.

Knock knock.
Who's there?
Emil.
Emil who?
Emil would be nice if you've got some foo<

Knock knock.
Who's there?
Ron.
Ron who?
Ron way round.

Knock knock.
Who's there?
Yul.
Yul who?
Yuletide.

Knock knock.
Who's there?
Ralph.
Ralph who?
Ralph, ralph - I'm just a puppy.

Knock knock.
Who's there?
Will.
Will who?
Will you go away?

Knock knock.
Who's there?
Alec.
Alec who?
Alec your sister but I
don't like you.

Knock knock.
Who's there?
Stan.
Stan who?
Stan back, I'm going to be sick.

❧

Knock knock.
Who's there?
Omar.
Omar who?
Omar goodness, what are you doing in there?

❧

Knock knock.
Who's there?
Eamon.
Eamon who?
Eamon a good mood - have my piece of cake.

Knock knock.
Who's there?
Aaron.
Aaron who?
Aaron'd boy, of course!

❧

Knock knock.
Who's there?
Nick.
Nick who?
Nick R. Elastic.

❧

Knock knock.
Who's there?
Ahmed.
Ahmed who?
Ahmed a big mistake coming here!

Lyle low until the cops have

Knock knock.
Who's there?
Murray.
Murray who?
Murray me now.

Knock knock.
Who's there?
Greg.
Greg who?
Greg scott!

Knock knock.
Who's there?
Alan.
Alan who?
Alan a good cause.

Knock knock.
Who's there?
Roland.
Roland who?
Roland stone gathers
no moss.

Knock knock.
Who's there?
Pierre.
Pierre
who?
Pierre
through
the
keyhole
- you'll
see.

Knock knock. Who's there?
Jack. Jack who?
Jack in the box.

Knock knock.
Who's there?
Noah.
Noah who?
Noah don't know who
you are either.

Knock knock.
Who's there?
Hiram.
Hiram who?
Hiram and fire 'em.

Knock knock.
Who's there?
Alexander.
Alexander who?
Alexander friend
want to come over.

Knock knock.
Who's there?
Ray.
Ray who?
Rayning cats and dogs.

↗

Knock knock.
Who's there?
Bjorn.
Bjorn who?
Bjorn free.

↗

Knock knock.
Who's there?
Russell.
Russell who?
Russelling leaves.

↗

Knock knock.
Who's there?
Sid.
Sid who?
Sid on it!

Knock knock.
Who's there?
Leon.
Leon who?
Leon me -
I'll support you.

Knock knock.
Who's there?
Sonny.
Sonny who?
Sonny outside, isn't it?

Knock knock.
Who's there?
Luke.
Luke who?
Luke warm.

Knock knock.
Who's there?
Troy.
Troy who?
Troy the
bell instead.

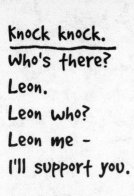
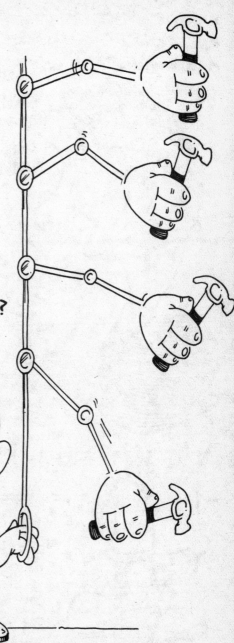

Knock knock.
Who's there?
Malcolm.
Malcolm who?
Malcolm outside
and play!

Knock knock.
Who's there?
Othello.
Othello who?
Othello I wouldn't trust an inch.

Who's there?

francis who?

Knock knock.
Who's there?
Duane.
Duane who?
Duane gonna get away
with dis!

Knock knock.
Who's there?
Walter.
Walter who?
Walter wall carpeting.

Knock knock. Who's there?
Ezra. Ezra who?
Ezra room for me to stay in?

Knock knock

francis

francis where
the french live

Knock knock.
Who's there?
Bert.
Bert who?
Bert the cakes.

Knock knock.
Who's there?
Alf.
Alf who?
If all if you don't catch me!

Knock knock.
Who's there?
Hayden.
Hayden who?
Hayden behind the door.

Knock knock.
Who's there?
Dwight.
Dwight who?
Dwight house is where
the president lives.

Knock knock.
Who's there?
Ian.
Ian who?
Ian a lot of money.

Knock knock.
Who's there?
Fletcher.
Fletcher who?
Fletcher stick, there's
a good boy.

Knock knock.
Who's there?
Howard.
Howard who?
Howard you know? You
won't even open up.

Knock knock.
Who's there?
Michael.
Michael who?
Michael beat you up if
you don't open the door.

Knock knock.
Who's there?
Ellis.
Ellis who?
Ellis damnation.

Knock knock.
Who's there?
Jason.
Jason who?
Jason a rainbow.

Knock knock.
Who's there?
Eli.
Eli who?
Elies all the time.

Knock knock.
Who's there?
Percy.
Percy who?
Percyverence is the
secret of success.

Knock knock.
Who's there?
Ethan.
Ethan who?
Ethan a chocolate bar.

Knock knock.
Who's there?
Gary.
Gary who?
Gary on smiling

Knock knock.
Who's there?
Alfie.
Alfie who?
Alfie terrible if you
leave.

◇   ◇

Knock knock.
Who's there?
Andy.
Andy who?
Andy man.

Knock knock.
Who's there?
Ellis.
Ellis who?
Ellis before 'M'.

_____

Knock knock.
Who's there?
Eddie.
Eddie who?
Eddie-body you like.

Who's there?

Isaac who?

Knock knock.
Who's there?
Brad.
Brad who?
Brad to meet
ya!

Knock knock.
Who's there?
Chester.
Chester who?
Chester
drawers.

Carlo.
Carlo who?
Carload of
junk.

Brendan.
Brendan who?
Brendan ear to what I have to say.

Knock knock.
Who's there?
Evan.
Evan who?
Evan only knows!

Knock knock.
Who's there?
Ewan.
Ewan who?
Ewan me should get
together.

KNOCK KNOCK WHO'S THERE?

Adam.
Adam who?
Adam nuisance come to
borrow some sugar.

Knock knock.
Who's there?
Frank.
Frank who?
Frank you very
much.

Knock knock.
Who's there?
Ben.
Ben who?
Ben down and
tie your
shoelaces.

Knock knock.
Who's there?
Caesar.
Caesar who?
Caesar arm to
stop her
getting away.

Knock knock.
Who's there?
Serena.
Serena who?
Serena round Saturn.

Knock knock.
Who's there?
Dale.
Dale who?
Dale come if you call dem.

Knock knock.
Who's there?.
Hugh who?
Hugh wouldn't believe it if I told you.

Knock knock.
Who's there?
Derek.
Derek who?
Derek get richer and the poor get poorer.

Knock knock.
Who's there?
Devlin.
Devlin who?
Devlin a red dress.

Knock knock.
Who's there?
Danny.
Danny who?
Dannybody home?

Knock knock.
Who's there?
Duncan.
Duncan who?
Duncan make your
garden grow.

Knock knock.
Who's there?
Darren.
Darren who?
Darren the garden,
hiding.

Knock knock.
Who's there?
Frank.
Frank who?
Frank you very much.

———

Knock knock.
Who's there?
Diego.
Diego who?
Diego before de 'B'.

———

Knock knock.
Who's there?
Desi.
Desi who?
Desi take sugar?

Knock knock

Kurt

Kurt and wounded

KNOCK KNOCK.

Don.
Don who?
Don take me
for granted.

Guthrie.
Guthrie who?
Guthrie ice-creams
in my hand.

Ivan.
Ivan who?
Ivan enormous snake
in my pocket.

WHO'S THERE?...

Ivor.

Ivor who?

Ivor lot more jokes where this came from!

Kenneth.

Kenneth who?

Kenneth three little kittens
come out to play?

o
Justin.

Justin who?

Justin time.

> Knock knock.
> Who's there?
> Paul.
> Paul who?
> Paul up a chair
> and I'll tell you.

Emmett.

Emmett who?

Emmett the front door,
not the back.

Knock knock.
Who's there?
Felix.
Felix who?
Felixtremely cold.

Knock knock.
Who's there?
Ray.
Ray who?
Ray drops keep
falling on my
head.

Knock knock.
Who's there?
Earl.
Earl who?
Earl tell you if you
open the door.

Knock knock.
Who's there?
Deduct.
Deduct who?
Donald Deduct.

Knock knock.
Who's there?
Felix.
Felix who?
Felix my ice-cream again I'll scream!

Knock knock.
Who's there?
Jeff.
Jeff who?
Jeff fancy
going out
tonight?

Knock knock.
Who's there?
Benjamin.
Benjamin who.
Benjamin the blues..

Knock knock.
Who's there?
Jeffrey.
Jeffrey who?
Jeffrey time I knock you ask who I am.

Knock knock.
Who's there?
Juan.
Juan who?
Juance upon a time
there were three
bears ....

Knock knock.
Who's there?
Jerry.
Jerry who?
Jerry cake.

Knock knock.
Who's there?
Jesse.
Jesse who?
Jesse if you can
recognize my voice.

Knock knock.
Who's there?
Wayne.
Wayne who?
(sing) "Wayne in a
manger, no crib for a
bed."

Knock knock.
Who's there?
Jess.
Jess who?
Jess li'l ol' me.

Who's there?

Jimmy who?

Knock knock.
Who's there?
Juan.
Juan who?
Just Juan of
those things.

Knock knock.
Who's there?
Cain.
Cain who?
Cain tell you.

Knock knock.
Who's there?
Robin.
Robin who?
Robin banks.

Knock knock.
Who's there?
Fred.
Fred who?
Fred this needle - I'm cross-eyed.

Knock knock.
Who's there?
Colin.
Colin who?
Colin and see me next time you're passing.

Who's there?

Romeo who?

Knock knock.
Who's there?
Joe.
Joe who?
Joe away –
I'm not talking
to you.

Knock knock.
Who's there?
Jude.
Jude who?
Jude doubt me? Just open up.

Knock knock.
Who's there?
Bernie.
Bernie who?
Bernie the dinner.

Knock knock.
Who's there?
Norman.
Norman who?
Norman behaviour
is expected here.

Knock knock.

Grant

Grant
three
wishes

Knock knock.
Who's there?
Albert.
Albert who?
Albert you'll never guess.

Knock knock.
Who's there?
Luke.
Luke who?
Luke through
the peep-hole
and you'll see.

Knock knock.
Who's there?
Evan.
Evan who?
Evan you should know
who it is.

Knock knock.
Who's there?
Paul.
Paul who?
Paul your weight!

?

Who's there?

Grant who?

Knock knock.
Who's there?
Ira.
Ira who?
Irate - or I will be if I
stand out here any longer!

KNOCK KNOCK

Knock knock.
Who's there?
Lewis.
Lewis who?
Lewis all my money in
a poker game.

Knock knock.
Who's there?
Cole.
Cole who?
Cole as a cucumber.

Knock knock.
Who's there?
Dog.
Dog who?
Doggedly standing at
your door.

Knock knock.
Who's there?
Alex.
Alex who?
Alexplain later if you let
me in.

Knock knock.
Who's there?
Musketeer.
Musketeer who?
Musketeer a doorbell -
I'm tired of knocking.

Knock knock.
Who's there?
Burglar.
Burglar who?
Burglars don't knock.

Knock knock.
Who's there?
Xavier.
Xavier who?
Xavier breath! I'm not
leaving.

Knock knock.
Who's there?
Esau.
Esau who?
Esau you in the bath!

Knock knock.
Who's there?
Parrot.
Parrot who?
Parrotly you live here.

Knock knock.
Who's there?
Tango.
Tango who?
Tango faster than this,
you know.

Knock knock.
Who's there?
Weevil.
Weevil who?
Weevil make you talk.

Knock knock.
Who's there?
Pepsi.
Pepsi who?
Pepsi through the peephole.

Knock knock.
Who's there?
Fanta.
Fanta who?
Fanta Claus.

Knock knock

Wicked

Wicked make
beautiful music
together.

Knock knock.
Who's there?
Kit Kat.
Kit Kat who?
Kit Kat is stuck
up the tree.

Knock knock.
Who's there?
Mars.
Mars who?
Marsays you've got to
come home now.

Knock knock.
Who's there?
Snickers.
Snickers who?
Snickers at me
because I'm small.

Knock knock.
Who's there?
Tic tac.
Tic tac who?
Tic tac paddy whack,
give the dog a bone.

Knock knock.
Who's there?
Topic.
Topic who?
Topic a wild-
flower is against
the law.

Knock knock.
Who's there?
Jelly Bean.
Jelly Bean who?
Jelly Bean to
the sea yet?

Knock knock.
Who's there?
Maltesers.
Maltesers who?
Maltesers the girls
terribly.

Knock knock.
Who's there?
Almond.
Almond who?
Almond come in,
I'm expected here.

Knock knock.
Who's there?
Truffle.
Truffle who?
Truffle with you is
you are so shy.

Knock knock.
Who's there?
Sherbert.
Sherbert who?
Sherbert to his room
- he's going to stay
for a couple of days.

"KNOCK" KNOCK

Doughnut.
Doughnut who?
Doughnut open the
door whatever
you do.

Chocs.
Chocs who?
Chocs away!

Toffee.
Toffee who?
Toffeel loved is the
best thing in
the world.

◇

Cookie.
Cookie who?
Cookien the
kitchen - it's
easier.

"WHO'S" THERE?

Knock knock.
Who's there?
Bun.
Bun who?
Bunnies make
the best pets.

Knock knock.
Who's there?
Lolly.
Lolly who?
Lollyng about
on the sofa.

Knock knock.
Who's there?
Ice-cream.
Ice-cream
who?
Ice-cream
louder than
anyone.

Knock knock.
Who's there?
fudge.
fudge who?
fudge up -
there's no room!

Knock knock.
Who's there?
Choc-ice.
Choc-ice who?
Choc-ice into this glass
would you?

Knock knock.
Who's there?
Nougat.
Nougat who?
Nougat can go
that fast!

Knock knock.
Who's there?
Tuba.
Tuba who?
Tuba toothpaste.

Knock knock.
Who's there?
Pastille.
Pastille who?
Pastille long
road you'll find
a village.

Knock knock.
Who's there?
Nestle.
Nestle who?
Nestle into
the soft
chair.

Knock knock.
Who's there?
cello.
cello who?
cello, how are
you?

Knock knock.
Who's there?
Violin.
Violin who?
Violin horrible
boy.

Knock knock.
Who's there?
Flute.
Flute who?
Flute in the
basement -
everything's
wet.

Knock knock.
Who's there?
Recorder.
Recorder who?
Recorder film for me
tonight, will you?

Knock knock.
Who's there?
organ.
organ who?
organize a party –
it's my birthday.

Knock knock.
Who's there?
Keyboard.
Keyboard who?
Keyboard today won't
work.

Knock knock.
Who's there?
oboe.
oboe who?
oboe! I've got the
wrong house!

Knock knock.
Who's there?
Fiddle.
Fiddle who?
Fiddle-di-dee.

Knock knock.
Who's there?
Drum.
Drum who?
Drum as fast as you
can.

Knock knock.
Who's there?
Doctor.
Doctor Who?
That's right - where's my Tardis?

Knock knock.
Who's there?
Cat.
Cat who?
Cat you
understand?

Knock knock.
Who's there?
Moth.
Moth who?
Motht get
mythelf a
key.

Knock knock.
Who's there?
Lettuce.
Lettuce who?
Lettuce in and we'll
tell you.

Knock knock.
Who's there?
Panther.
Panther who?
Panther what you
wear on your legth.

Knock knock.
Who's there?
Smee.
Smee who?
Smee, your
friend.

Knock knock.
Who's there?
Armageddon.
Armageddon who?
Armageddon out of
here quick.

Knock knock.
Who's there?
Bull.
Bull who?
Bull the chain.

Knock knock.
Who's there?
Pen.
Pen who?
Pent-up emotions!

Knock knock.
Who's there?
Basket.
Basket who?
Basket home, it's nearly
dark.

Knock knock.
Who's there?
Summer.
Summer who? Summer good, some are bad.

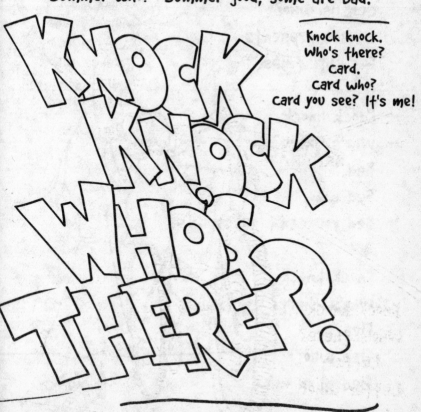

Knock knock.
Who's there?
Card.
Card who?
Card you see? It's me!

Knock knock.
Who's there?
Biro.
Biro who?
Biro light of the moon.

Knock knock.
Who's there?
Census.
Census who?
Census presents
for Christmas.

Knock knock.
Who's there?
Bed.
Bed who?
Bed you can't guess who.

Knock knock.
Who's there?
Flea.
Flea who?
Flea blind mice.

Knock knock.
Who's there?
Bug.
Bug who?
Bug Rogers.

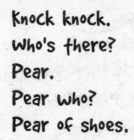

Knock knock.
Who's there?
Pear.
Pear who?
Pear of shoes.

Knock knock.
Who's there?
Shoes.
Shoes who?
Shoes me, I didn't
mean to steal your
pears.

Knock knock.
Who's there?
Leaf.
Leaf who?
Leaf me be!

Knock knock.
Who's there?
Lock.
Lock who?
Lock through
the peephole.

Knock knock.
Who's there?
Aitch.
Aitch who?
Bless you.

Knock knock.
Who's there?
Fang.
Fang who?
Fang you for
having me.

Knock knock.
Who's there?
Noise.
Noise who?
Noise to
see you.

Knock knock.

Wool

Wool you
marry me?

Knock knock.
Who's there?
Earwig.
Earwig who?
Earwigo!

Knock knock.
Who's there?
Tick.
Tick who?
Tick 'em up and gimme
all your money.

Knock knock.
Who's there?
Canoe.
Canoe who?
Canoe lend me a fiver?

Knock knock.
Who's there?
Diesel.
Diesel who?
Diesel make you feel
better.

◇ ◇

Knock knock.
Who's there?
Dish.
Dish who?
Dish ish a shtick-up!

Knock knock.
Who's there?
Me.
Me who?
I didn't know you had
a cat!

◇ ◇

Knock knock.
Who's there?
Dozen.
Dozen who?
Dozen anyone know
my name?

162

Knock knock.
Who's there?
Snow.
Snow who?
Snow business of yours.

◇

Knock knock.
Who's there?
Nanny.
Nanny who?
Nanny-one home?

◇

Knock knock.
Who's there?
Oz.
Oz who?
Oz got something for you.

◇

Knock knock.
Who's there?
Kiwi.
Kiwi who?
Kiwit any longer.

Dishwasher.
Dishwasher who?
Dishwasher way I shpoke before I had my teef fixshed.

Knock knock.
Who's there?
Thistle.
Thistle who?
Thistle be the last
time I knock.

Knock knock.
Who's there?
Ammonia.
Ammonia who?
Ammonia poor boy,
nobody loves me.

Knock knock.
Who's there?
Avon.
Avon who?
Avon calling - your
bell's broken.

Knock knock.
Who's there?
Furry.
Furry who?
Furry's a jolly good
fellow!

Knock knock.
Who's there?
Fish.
Fish who?
Bless you!

Knock knock.
Who's there?
Small man.
Small man who?
Small man who can't
reach the doorbell.

Knock knock.
Who's there?
Canon.
Canon who?
Canon open the door
then?

Knock knock.
Who's there?
Oil.
Oil who?
Oil be seeing you.

━ o ━

Knock knock.
Who's there?
Pencil.
Pencil who?
Pencil fall down if your
belt snaps.

━ o ━

Knock knock.
Who's there?
Dutch.
Dutch who?
Dutch my hands -
they're freezing.

━ o ━

Knock knock.
Who's there?
Kipper.
Kipper who?
Kipper your hands to
yourself.

Knock knock.
Who's there?
Atomic.
Atomic who?
Atomic ache - cause
I've eaten too much.

━ o ━

Knock knock.
Who's there?
Money.
Money who?
Money is hurting - I
knocked it playing
football.

━ o ━

Knock knock.
Who's there?
Cattle.
Cattle who?
Cattle purr if you
stroke it.

━ o ━

Butter.
Butter who?
Butter hurry up, I need the toilet now!

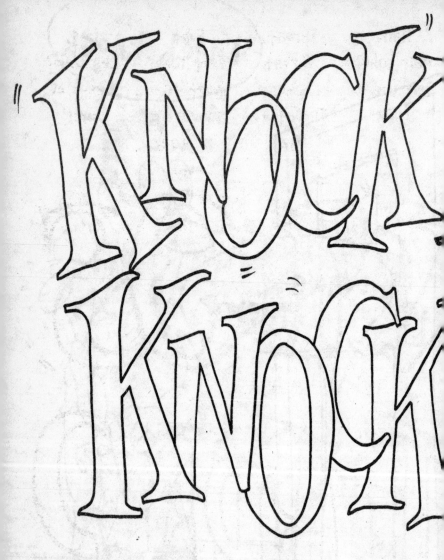

"KNOCK KNOCK
KNOCK KNOCK"

Eye.	Ear.	Nose.	Chest.
Eye who?	Ear who?	Nose who?	Chest who?
Eye know	Ear you	Nosinging	Chestnuts
who you	are - a	in the	for sale!
are.	letter.	house.	

Hair.
Hair who?
Hair we go
again.

Throat.
Throat
who?
Throat to
me.

Foot.
Foot who?
Foot two
pence I'd
go away
now.

Leg.
Leg who?
Leggo of
me!

"WHO'S"
THERE?

Knock knock.
Who's there?
Thumb.
Thumb who?
Thumb like it hot.

Knock knock.
Who's there?
Ears.
Ears who?
Ears looking at you kid.

Knock knock.
Who's there?
Knee.
Knee who?
Kneed you ask?

Knock knock.
Who's there?
Thighs.
Thighs who?
Thighs the limit.

Knock knock.
Who's there?
Knees.
Knees who?
Knees you every day.

Knock knock.
Who's there?
Tooth.
Tooth who?
Tooth or dare.

Knock knock.
Who's there?
Paris.
Paris who?
Paris the pepper please.

Knock knock.
Who's there?
Glasgow.
Glasgow who?
Glasgow to the movies.

Knock knock.   Who's there?

Mecca.   Kyoto.
Mecca who?   Kyoto who?
Mecca my day!   Kyoto town tonight!

Knock knock,

Who's there?

Moscow

Moscow who?

Moscow home soon.

Knock knock.
Who's there?
Minsk.
Minsk who?
Minsk meat.

Knock knock.
Who's there?
Munich.
Munich who?
Munich some money
for me?

Knock knock.
Who's there?
Teheran.
Teheran who?
Teheran and look me
in the eye.

Knock knock.
Who's there?
Lisbon.
Lisbon who?
Lisbon away a long
time.

Knock knock.
Who's there?
Perth.
Perth who?
Perth full of money.

Turin.
Turin who?
Turin to a werewolf under a full moon.

Knock knock.
Who's there?
Greece.
Greece who?
Greece my palm and I'll
tell you.

Knock knock.
Who's there?
Crete.
Crete who?
Crete to see you.

Knock knock.
Who's there?
Cyprus.
Cyprus who?
Cyprus the bell?

Knock knock.
Who's there?
Havana.
Havana who?
Havana great time
here!

Knock knock.
Who's there?
Ghent.
Ghent who?
Ghent out of town.

Knock knock.
Who's there?
Delhi.
Delhi who?
Delhi a joke ....

Knock knock.
Who's there?
Athens.
Athens who?
Athenshadow over the
moon.

Knock knock.
Who's there?
Chad.
Chad who?
Chad you could come.

Knock knock.
Who's there?
Haiti.
Haiti who?
Haitit when you
talk like that!

Knock knock.
Who's there?
Belize.
Belize who?
oh, Belize yourself
then.

Knock knock.
Who's there?
Cologne.
Cologne who?
Cologne around the
world and meet
people.

Knock knock.
Who's there?
Sweden.
Sweden who?
Sweden the pill.

Knock knock.
Who's there?
Chile.
Chile who?
Chile without your
coat on!

Knock knock. Who's there?
Egypt. Egypt who?
Egypt me out in the cold!

Knock knock.
Who's there?
Cuba.
Cuba who?
Cuba wood.

Knock knock.
Who's there?
Kenya.
Kenya who?
Kenya guess?

Knock knock.
Who's there?
Guinea.
Guinea who?
Guinea a high five!

Knock knock.
Who's there?
Congo.
Congo who?
Congo into town - it's
dangerous.

Knock knock.
Who's there?
Benin.
Benin who?
Benin a good mood
lately.

Knock knock.
Who's there?
Uganda.
Uganda who?
Uganda go away now?

Knock knock.
Who's there?
Pill.
Pill who?
Pill you open the
door?

Knock knock.
Who's there?
Pizza.
Pizza
who?
Pizza
this,
piece of that.

Knock knock.
Who's there?
Razor.
Razor who?
Razor laugh at that
joke.

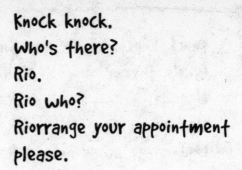

Knock knock.
Who's there?
Rio.
Rio who?
Riorrange your appointment
please.

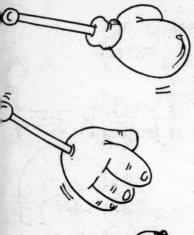

Knock knock.
Who's there?
Berlin.
Berlin who?
Berlint me some books.

Knock knock.
Who's there?
Peru.
Peru who?
Peruse this map before
you go.

Knock knock.
Who's there?
Seville.
Seville who?
Seville oranges.

KNOCK WHO'S KNOCK THERE?

Galway.

Galway who?

Galway you silly boy.

Dublin.

Dublin who?

Dublin up with laughter.

Alaska.

Alaska who?

Alaska one more time.

Knock knock.
Who's there?

Brighton.
Brighton who?
Brighton this side of the mountain.

Hawaii.	florida.	Utah.	Iowa.
Hawaii who?	florida who?	Utah who?	Iowa who?
Hawaii getting on?	florida room is sticky.	Utah'ld me to come round.	Iowa lot to you.

KNOCK KNOCK KNOCK KNOCK KNOCK KNOCK

THERE?

Missouri.
Missouri
who?
Missouri
me!

Maine.
Maine
who?
Maine
reason I'm
here!

Brazil.
Brazil
who?
Brazil hold
your
breasts
up.

Russia.
Russia
who?
Russia
little
more if
you want
to get
there on
time.

183

Knock knock.
Who's there?
Bolivia.
Bolivia who?
Bolivia me, I know what I'm talking about.
◌
Knock knock.
Who's there?
Jamaica.
Jamaica who?
Jamaica mistake?
◌
Knock knock.
Who's there?
Europe.
Europe who?
Europening the door
very slowly.
◌
Knock knock.
Who's there?
Ann.
Ann who?
Ann Tarctic.

Knock knock.

Knock knock.
Who's there?
Amazon.
Amazon who?
Amazon very bad mood.

Knock knock.
Who's there?
Asia.
Asia who?
Asia mother in?

Knock knock.
Who's there?
Czech.
Czech who?
Czech and see!

Who's there?

Knock knock.
Who's there?
Norway.
Norway who?
Norway is this your
house - it's too grand!

Knock knock.
Who's there?
Bosnia.
Bosnia who?
Bosnia bell here
earlier?

Knock knock.
Who's there?
Venice.
Venice who?
Venice this going to
end?

Knock knock.
Who's there?
Rome.
Rome who?
Roming around.

Knock knock.
Who's there?
Madrid.
Madrid who?
Madrid you
wash my
sports
kit?

Knock knock.
Who's there?
Sienna.
Sienna who?
Siennathing good at the movies?

Knock knock.
Who's there?
Tennis.
Tennis who?
Tennis two times five.

Knock knock.
Who's there?
Ghana.
Ghana who?
Ghana get me a gun and go into town.

WET PAINT

Knock knock.
Who's there?
Spain.
Spain who?
Spaint all over the wall!

Knock knock.
Who's there?
Iran.
Iran who?
Iran all the way home.

Knock knock.
Who's there?
Iraq.
Iraq who?
Iraq of lamb for
dinner, please.

Knock knock.
Who's there?
Ireland.
Ireland who?
Ireland is the best
land in the world.

Knock knock.
Who's there?
Denmark.
Denmark who?
Denmark your own
territory.

Knock knock.
Who's there?
Hand.
Hand who?
Handover your money.

Knock knock.
Who's there?
Tummy.
Tummy who?
Tummy you'll always be
the best.

Knock knock.
Who's there?
Spider.
Spider who?
Spider across the road.

Knock knock.
Who's there?
Hip.
Hip who?
Hippopotamus.

Knock knock.
Who's there?
Uncle.
Uncle who?
Uncle Arthur.
Knock knock.
Who's there?
Uncle.

Uncle who?
Uncle Arthur.
Knock knock.
Who's there?
Auntie.
Auntie who?
Auntie glad it's
not Uncle
Arthur?

...and that's for not opening the door!

Knock knock.
Who's there?
Gran.
Gran who?
Grant me three
wishes.

◇   ◇

Knock knock.
Who's there?
Sis.
Sis who?
Sistine chapel of
course.

◇   ◇

Knock knock.
Who's there?
Brother.
Brother who?
Brotheration! I've
forgotten my own
name!

◇   ◇

Knock knock.
Who's there?
Owl.
Owl who?
Owl I can say is knock
knock.

◇   ◇

Knock knock.
Who's there?
Butcher.
Butcher who?
Butcher left leg in,
your left leg out ....

◇   ◇

Knock knock.
Who's there?
House.
House who?
Hugh's fine thanks.
How's John?

◇   ◇

Knock knock. Who's there?
Dad. Dad who?
Dadda! Lets have a red carpet out!

Knock knock.
Who's there?
Mum.
Mum who?
Mum's the word.

Knock knock.
Who's there?
Baby.
Baby who?
(sing) "Baby love, my baby love...."

Knock knock.
Who's there?
Nanny.
Nanny who?
Nanny people are waiting to come in.

Knock knock.
Who's there?
Cousin.
Cousin who?
Cousin stead of opening the door you're leaving me here.

Knock knock.
Who's there?
Thumping.
Thumping who?
Thumping's jutht knocked my teef out.

Knock knock.
Who's there?
Police.
Police who?
Police open the door.

Knock knock.
Who's there?
Boo.
Boo who?
Oh please don't cry!

Knock knock.
Who's there?
Too whit.
Too whit who?
Is there an owl in the house?

Knock knock.
Who's there?
You.
You who?
Who's that calling out?

Knock knock.
Who's there?
Wooden shoe.
Wooden shoe who?
Wooden shoe like to
know?

Knock knock.
Who's there?
Sloane.
Sloane who?
Sloanely outside
- let me in.

Knock knock.
Who's there?
Little old lady.
Little old lady who?
I didn't know you could yodel.

Knock knock.
Who's there?
Pizza.
Pizza who?
Pizza the action.

Knock knock.
Who's there?
Chrome.
Chrome who?
Chromosome.

Knock knock.
Who's there?
Yoga.
Yoga who?
Yoga what it takes!

Knock knock.
Who's there?
Hosanna.
Hosanna who?
Hosanna claus gets down our tiny chimney I'll never know!

Knock knock.
Who's there?
March.
March who?
March, march, quick, quick, march.

~~~~~~~~~~~~~~~~~~~~~~~~~~~~~~~~~~~~

Knock knock.
Who's there?
Collie.
Collie who?
Collie Miss Molly, I don't know

~~~~~~~~~~~~~~~~~~~~~~~~~~~~~~~~~~~~

Knock knock.
Who's there?
Bark.
Bark who?
Bark your car in the garage.

~~~~~~~~~~~~~~~~~~~~~~~~~~~~~~~~~~~~

Knock knock.
Who's there?
Howl.
Howl who?
Howl I know when it's supper time?

Knock knock.
Who's there?
Pudding.
Pudding who?
Pudding our best feet forward.

Knock knock.
Who's there?
May.
May who?
May I come in?

Knock knock.
Who's there?
June.
June who?
Juneo what time it is?

Knock knock.

Who's there?

April

April who?

April will make you feel better

Knock knock. Who's there?
Jewel. Jewel who?
Jewel know me when you open the door.

Knock knock

Distress

Distress is
brand new

Knock knock.
Who's there?
Denial.
Denial who?
Denial flows through Egypt.

◇

Knock knock.
Who's there?
Disk.
Disk who?
Diskusting!

Knock knock.
Who's there?
Mountain.
Mountain who?
Mountain debts.

Knock knock.
Who's there?
Mustard.
Mustard who?
Mustard left it in the car.

Who's there?

Distress who?

Knock knock.
Who's there?
July.
July who?
July or do you tell the truth?

Knock knock.
Who's there?
August.
August who?
August go away, shall I?

Knock knock.
Who's there?
Nobody.
Nobody who?
.... just nobody.

Knock knock.
Who's there?
Pecan.
Pecan who?
Pecan boo!

Knock knock.
Who's there?
Pasta.
Pasta who?
Pasta salt please.

Knock knock.
Who's there?
Phone.
Phone who?
Phoney I'd known
it was you.

Knock knock.
Who's there?
Scold.
Scold who?
Scold outside. Please let me in.

Knock knock.
Who's there?
Puss.
Puss who.
Puss the door –
it won't open.

Knock knock.
Who's there?
Dish.
Dish who?
Dish ish shilly.

Knock knock.
Who's there?
Fork.
Fork who?
Forket her – she
wasn't worth it.

Knock knock.
Who's there?
Chicken.
Chicken who?
Chicken your pockets
- I think your keys
are there.

Knock knock.
Who's there?
Bowl.
Bowl who?
Bowl me over.

Knock knock.
Who's there?
Bacon.
Bacon who?
Bacon a cake in the oven.

Knock knock.
Who's there?
Apple.
Apple who?
Apple the door
myself.

Knock knock.
Who's there?
Egg.
Egg who?
Eggsactly.

Knock knock.
Who's there?
Soup.
Soup who?
Souper Man!

Knock knock.
Who's there?
Butter.
Butter who?
Butter wrap up –
it's cold out here.

Knock knock.
Who's there?
Ketchup.
Ketchup who?
Ketchup the tree.

Knock knock.
Who's there?
Marmalade.
Marmalade who?
Marmalade an egg
for me.

Knock knock.
Who's there?
Wine.
Wine who?
Wine now you are
all grown up!

Knock knock.
Who's there?
Juice.
Juice who?
Juice still want
to know?

Knock knock.
Who's there?
Tuna.
Tuna who?
Tuna whole orchestra.

Knock knock.
Who's there?
Curry.
Curry who?
Curry me all the way.

Knock knock.
Who's there?
Parsley.
Parsley who?
Parsley jam please.

Knock knock.
Who's there?
Beef.
Beef who?
Beef fair

Who's there?

Kanga who?

Knock knock.
Who's there?
Fig.
Fig who?
Figs the step,
it's broken.

KNOCK KNOCK

Knock knock.
Who's there?
fruit.
fruit who?
fruit of all evil.

Knock knock.
Who's there?
Goose.
Goose who?
Goosee what's the matter.

Knock knock

Kanga

No, Kangaroo

WHO'S THERE?

Knock knock.
Who's there?
Mint.
Mint who?
Mint to tell you earlier.

Knock knock.
Who's there?
Muffin.
Muffin who?
Muffin to declare.

Knock knock.
Who's there?
Peas.
Peas who?
Peas to meet you.

Knock knock.
Who's there?
Pecan.
Pecan who?
Pecan work it out.

Knock knock.
Who's there?
Jam.
Jam who?
Jam mind! I'm trying
to think out here.

Knock knock.
Who's there?
Tarzan.
Tarzan who?
Tarzan stripes
forever!

Knock knock.
Who's there?
Quebec.
Quebec who?
Quebec there
if you want a
ticket.

Knock knock.
Who's there?
Vampire.
Vampire who?
Vampire state building.

Knock knock.
Who's there?
Cereal.
Cereal who?
Cereal pleasure to
meet you.

—

Knock knock.
Who's there?
Ward.
Ward who?
Ward you want?

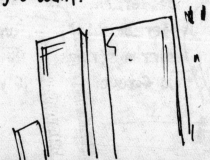

Knock knock.
Who's there?
Dakota.
Dakota who?
Dakota is too small
round the neck.

Knock knock.
Who's there?
Delta.
Delta who?
Delta great hand
of cards.

Knock knock.
Who's there?
Visa.
Visa who?
Visa the ones
you want.

Knock knock.
Who's there?
Gorilla.
Gorilla who?
Gorilla sausage.

Knock knock.
Who's there?
Jester.
Jester who?
Jester silly
old man.

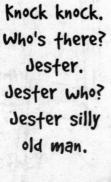

Knock knock.
Who's there?
Vault.
Vault who?
Vaultzing Matilda.

Knock knock.
Who's there?
King.
King who?
Kingy boots!

Knock knock.
Who's there?
Queen.
Queen who?
Queen of the crop.

Knock knock.
Who's there?
Fantasy.
Fantasy who?
Fantasy meeting
you the other day.

Knock knock.
Who's there?
Duke.
Duke who?
Duke come here often?

✗

Knock knock.
Who's there?
Load.
Load who?
Loadsamoney.

Knock knock.
Who's there?
Voodoo.
Voodoo who?
Voodoo you think you
are?

Knock knock.
Who's there?
Spell.
Spell who?
Spelling is easy when
you know how.

Knock knock.
Who's there?
Royal.
Royal who?
Royal show you
his paintings if
you ask nicely.

Knock knock.
Who's there?
White.
White who?
White in the
middle of it.

Knock knock.
Who's there?
Orange.
Orange who?
Orange your day to suit the weather.

Knock knock.
Who's there?
Brown.
Brown who?
Brown, Charlie Brown.

Knock knock.
Who's there?
Grey.
Grey who?
Greyt balls of fire!

Knock Knock
Who's there?

Knock knock.
Who's there?
Magenta.
Magenta who?
Magenta with great
caution.

Knock knock.
Who's there?
Yellow.
Yellow who?
Yellowver the din - I
can't hear you.

Knock knock.
Who's
there?
Doll.
Doll who?
Dollet me
in, please?

Knock knock.
Who's there?
Cream.
Cream who?
Cream louder so the police
will come.

216

Knock knock.
Who's there?
Fax.
Fax who?
Fax you very much.

Knock knock.
Who's there?
Myth.
Myth who?
Myth Thmith, thilly!

Knock knock

Few

Few! What's that smell!

Knock knock.
Who's there?
Scar.
Scar who?
Scar will not go any faster.

Knock knock.
Who's there?
Dismay.
Dismay who?
Dismay surprise you but I'm from New York.

Knock knock.
Who's there?
Ryder.
Ryder who?
Ryder fast horse.

Knock knock.
Who's there?
Keanu.
Keanu who?
Keanu lend me a fiver?

Knock knock.
Who's there?
Diaz.
Diaz who?
Diaz of our lives.

~~~~~~~~~~~~~~~~~~~~~~~~

Knock knock.
Who's there?
Truman.
Truman who?
Truman and honest men are needed
for the jury.

~~~~~~~~~~~~~~~~~~~~~~~~

Knock knock.
Who's there?
Sondheim.
Sondheim who?
Sondheim soon we'll meet again.

~~~~~~~~~~~~~~~~~~~~~~~~

Knock knock.
Who's there?
Amin.
Amin who?
Amin man.

Knock knock.
Who's there?
Churchill.
Churchill who?
Churchill be the best place to get married.

Knock knock.
Who's there?
Rothschild.
Rothschild who?
Rothschild is very clever.

Knock knock.
Who's there?
Wedgwood.
Wedgwood who?
Wedgwood come if he could but he's busy.

Knock knock.
Who's there?
Grimm.
Grimm who?
Grimm and bear it.

Knock knock.
Who's there?
Bhuto.
Bhuto who?
Bhuton the other foot.

× × × ×

Knock knock.
Who's there?
Khomeini.
Khomeini who?
Khomeini time you like.

× × × ×

Knock knock.
Who's there?
Saddam.
Saddam who?
Saddam I that you couldn't come
to the party.

× × × ×

Knock knock.
Who's there?
Parton.
Parton who?
Parton my intrusion.

Knock knock.
Who's there?
Lumley.
Lumley who.
Lumley cakes!

Knock knock.
Who's there?
Stalin.
Stalin who?
Stalin for time.

Knock knock.
Who's there?
Borg.
Borg who?
Borg standard.

Knock knock.
Who's there?
MCEnroe.
MCEnroe who?
MCEnroe his boat fast.

Knock knock.
Who's there?
Chapman.
Chapman who?
Chapmany times if you like the show.

Knock knock.
Who's there?
Becker.
Becker who?
Becker the devil you know.

Knock knock.
Who's there?
Cher.
Cher who?
Cher and share alike!

Knock knock.

Who's there?

Spice.

Spice who?

Spice satellites are orbiting the earth.

Knock knock.

Who's there?

Madonna.

Madonna who?

Madonna's being mean - tell her off!

Knock knock.

Who's there?

Clark.

Clark who?

Clark your car out here.

Knock knock.

Who's there?

Kent.

Kent who?

Kent see without my glasses.

Knock knock.
Who's there?
Zippy.
Zippy who?
Zippy-dee-doo-dah, Zip-a-dee-day.

Knock knock.
Who's there?
Major.
Major who?
Major answer the door, didn't I?

Knock knock.
Who's there?
Frankenstein.
Frankenstein who?
Frankenstein his own name now.

Knock knock.
Who's there?
Fergie.
Fergie who?
Fergiedness sake let me in!

Knock knock.
Who's there?
Kylie.
Kylie who?
Kyliet your dog out for a walk?

Knock knock.
Who's there?
Bach.
Bach who?
Bach to work.

Knock knock.
Who's there?
Chopin.
Chopin who?
Chopin the department store.

Knock knock.
Who's there?
Mozart.
Mozart who?
Mozart is very beautiful.

Debussy.
Debussy
who?
Debussy's
never on
time.

Handel.
Handel
who?
Handel
with care.

Verdi.
Verdi who?
Verdia
want to
go?

Joplin.
Joplin
who?
Joplin any
time you
like.

Knock

Haydn.
Haydn
who?
Haydn the
shed.

Boyzone.
Boyzone
who?
Boyzone
adven-
tures.

UB40.
UB40
who?
UB40
today –
happy
birthday!

Donovan.
Donovan
who?
Donovan
the door
– it's
dangerous.

there?

229

Knock knock.
Who's there?
Morrissey.
Morrissey
who?
Morrissey the
pretty birdies?

Knock knock.
Who's there?
Billy Bragg.
Billy Bragg
who?
Billy Braggs too
much – tell
him to stop.

Knock knock.
Who's there?
Courtney Pine.
Courtney Pine
who?
Courtney Pine
tables? I want
to buy one.

Knock knock.
Who's there?
Metallica.
Metallica who?
Metallicand sleek looks are the
best for cars.

◇

Knock knock.
Who's there?
Bjork.
Bjork who?
Bjork in the USSR.

◇   ◇

Knock knock.
Who's there?
Demi Moore.
Demi Moore who?
Demi Moore than you did last time?

◇   ◇   ◇

Knock knock.
Who's there?
Depp.
Depp who?
Depp inside, dear!

Knock knock.
Who's there?
Warner.
Warner who?
Warner lift?
My car's outside.

Knock knock.
Who's there?
Supergrass.
Supergrass who?
Supergrass on
your lawn!

Knock knock.

Watson

Watson
your head.
It looks
silly.

Knock knock.
Who's there?
Sherlock.
Sherlock who?
Sherlock your
door - someone
could break in.

Knock knock.
Who's there?
Blur.
Blur who?
Blur! It's cold
out here.

Knock knock.
Who's there?
oasis.
oasis who?
oasis! Let your brother in!

Who's there?
Watson who?

Knock knock.
Who's there?
Abba.
Abba who?
Abba'out turn! Quick march!

Knock knock.
Who's there?
Pulp.
Pulp who?
Pulp pretty hard on the door - it's stiff.

Knock knock.
Who's there?
Stones.
Stones who?
Stones sober.

Knock knock.
Who's there?
Jagger.
Jagger who?
Jaggered edge.

Knock knock.
Who's there?
Sheryl crow.
Sheryl crow
who?
Sheryl crow
to the
movies tonight?

Knock knock. Who's there?
Bolton. Bolton who?
Bolton braces.

Knock knock.
Who's there?
Whitney.
Whitney who?
Whitneyssed the crime.

Knock knock.
Who's there?
Elton.
Elton who?
Elton old lady please.

Knock knock.
Who's there?
Mao.
Mao who?
Maothfull of toffee.

Knock knock.
Who's there?
De Niro.
De Niro who?
De Niro you get, the
faster I run.

Knock knock.
Who's there?
Pfeiffer.
Pfeiffer who?
Pfeiffer hours to
Australia.

Knock knock.
Who's there?
Ben Hur.
Ben Hur who?
Ben Hur an hour - le
me in.

Knock knock.
Who's there?
Thatcher.
Thatcher who?
Thatcher car? What a pile o

Knock knock.
Who's there?
Eisenhower.
Eisenhower who?
Eisenhower late for
work.

Knock knock.
Who's there?
Turner.
Turner who?
Turner handle and open
the door.

Knock knock.
Who's there?
Heywood.
Heywood who?
Heywood you
open the door?

Knock knock.
Who's there?
DiMaggio.
DiMaggio who?
DiMaggion yourself on a deserted island ....

~~~~~~

Knock knock.
Who's there?
Fonda.
Fonda who?
Fonda my family.

~~~~~~

Knock knock.
Who's there?
Harlow.
Harlow who?
Harlow can you get?

~~~~~~

Knock knock.
Who's there?
Gable.
Gable who?
Gable and Wireless.

~~~~~~

Knock knock.
Who's there?
olivier.
olivier who?
olivier all my money in my will.

Knock knock.
Who's there?
Kismet.
Kismet who?
Kismet quick!

Knock knock.
Who's there?
Manchu.
Manchu who?
Manchu your
food six times.

Knock knock.
Who's there?
Moses.
Moses who?
Moses the lawn.

Knock knock.
Who's there?
Noah.
Noah who?
Noah counting for taste.

Knock knock.
Who's there?
Ninja.
Ninja who?
Ninja with me every
day.

Knock knock.
Who's there?
Hardy.
Hardy who?
Hardy annual.

Knock knock.
Who's there?
Greene.
Greene who?
Greene is my valley.

Knock knock.
Who's there?
Bronte.
Bronte who?
Bronte of the blow.

Knock knock.
Who's there?
Austen.
Austen who?
Austentatiously rich.

Knock knock.
Who's there?
Forster.
Forster who?
Forstern issue.

Knock knock.
Who's there?
Woolf.
Woolf who?
Woolf in sheep's
clothing.

Byron.
Byron
who?
Byron new
suit.

Keats.
Keats
who?
Keats you
warm in
the
winter.

Gaskill.
Gaskill
who?
Gaskills if
it's not
turned
off.

Wilde.
Wilde
who?
Wilde at
heart.

Euripides.
Euripides
who?
Euripides,
you pay
for a new
pair.

Gopher.
Gopher
who?
Gopher
help - I'm
stuck in
the mud.

Orson.
Orson
who?
Orson, let
your daddy
in.

Harrison.
Harrison
who?
Harrison is
a credit
to his
father.

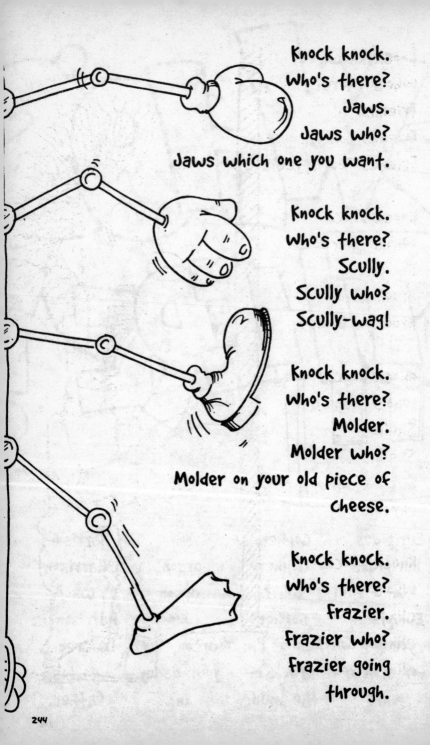

Knock knock.
Who's there?
Jaws.
Jaws who?
Jaws which one you want.

Knock knock.
Who's there?
Scully.
Scully who?
Scully-wag!

Knock knock.
Who's there?
Molder.
Molder who?
Molder on your old piece of
cheese.

Knock knock.
Who's there?
Frazier.
Frazier who?
Frazier going
through.

Knock knock.
Who's there?
friends.
friends who?
friends-ied attack.

Knock knock.
Who's there?
Brook.
Brook who?
Brooklyn Bridge.

Knock knock.
Who's there?
Sheilds.
Sheilds who?
Sheilds say
anything.

Knock knock.
Who's there?
Clinton.
Clinton who?
Clinton your eye.

Knock knock.
Who's there?
Blair.
Blair who?
Blair play.

Knock knock.
Who's there?
Gandhi.
Gandhi who?
Gandhi come out to play?

Knock knock.
Who's there?
Che.
Che who?
Che what you're made of.

Knock knock.
Who's there?
Lineker.
Lineker who?
Linekers in a big traffic jam.

Knock knock.
Who's there?
Gazza.
Gazza who?
Gazza kiss.

Knock knock.
Who's there?
Hobbit.
Hobbit who?
Hobbit-forming.

Knock knock.
Who's there?
Kermit.
Kermit who?
Kermit a crime and
you go to jail.

Knock knock.
Who's there?
Miss Piggy.
Miss Piggy
who?
Miss Piggy
went to
market, Miss
Piggy stayed
at home ....

MARKET

Knock knock.
Who's there?
Tele.
Tele who?
Tele your friend to come out.

Knock knock.
Who's there?
Tubby.
Tubby who?
Tubby or not to be.

Knock knock.
Who's there?
Ben and Anna.
Ben and Anna who?
Ben and Anna split.

Knock knock.
Who's there?
Al and Eady.
Al and Eady who?
Al and Eady's love.

Knock knock.
Who's there?
Stan and Della.
Stan and Della who?
Stan and Dellaver.

Knock knock.
Who's there?
Paul and Portia.
Paul and Portia who?
Paul and Portia door to open it.

Knock knock.
Who's there?
Freddie and Abel.
Freddie and Abel who?
Freddie and Abel to do business.

Knock knock.
Who's there?
Truman and Goode.
Truman and Goode who?
Twelve Truman and Goode for the jury.

Knock knock.
Who's there?
Stan and Bea.
Stan and Bea who?
Stan and Bea counted.

Knock knock.
Who's there?
Sheik and Geisha.
Sheik and Geisha who?
Sheik and Geisha'll find.

Knock knock.
Who's there?
Mike and Angelo
Mike and Angelo who?
Mike and Angelo's David.

Knock knock.
Who's there?
Crock and Dial
Crock and Dial who?

Crock and Dial
Dundee.